MW00877720

Tarot in the Modern World

TABLE OF CONTENTS

INTRODUCTION

Born into a psychic family, I was introduced to the Tarot by my Russian grandmother. Over 30 years and thousands of readings later, I have developed my own meanings for the cards.

Over the years I have noticed certain patterns and configurations inevitably mean certain things. This book will show you how to get a deeper understanding of the Tarot. We will go beyond memorizing the meaning of each card, and set you on the path of making the reading your own.

I do give interpretations for in card in the upright and reverse. These are all my personal interpretations that I have developed over the years. Some are quite conventional. Others are quite different from the traditional meanings. Updated for the 21st century, I include some modern interpretations of these ancient cards.

This book will show you how to tie the cards together into a cohesive reading. By sharing my findings with you, I hope to open your eyes to a different way of looking at the Tarot. Let us open the door to you discovering of your own meanings in these magical cards.

Vickie Verlie - www.youtube.com/rocknrollprophetess

LAYING THE CARDS

Every time I throw the cards they tell me a story.
I don't get too hung up on spreads and what each
placement means. It a story, and I have to throw
as many cards as it takes to tell the story.

Generally I do begin with a Celtic Cross, but very
seldom do I stop at 10 cards. No two readings are
alike, therefore the amount of cards thrown
varies as well. I never use a significator
(court card to represent the person) at the onset.
I would rather see where they fall out in the spread.
Where the significator ends up in the spread,
and the cards around it, can give great insight to the
to the reading. When asking about a specific person,
I will often keep throwing the cards until that person's
significator appears. The cards surrounding it can be
quite insightful and aid in timing. The further out they
are, the further away they may be.

If the person's significator does show up in the initial
spread, what cards are around them? These cards will
be key in telling the story. The Court Cards that face
in one direction are particularly noteworthy.
What are they looking at? This is the direction they
are headed, or a desire that they have. What are they
turned away from? This is something that they are
leaving behind, or literally don't want to face.
This is true with any cards that face in one direction,
not only the Court Cards.

A reading is more than each card alone.
You have to tie it together in order for it to make
sense to the seeker. So how do we go about this?
It does involve a fair amount of intuition.
If you want to take it to the next level you are going
to have to start taking chances and trusting.

When you throw the cards take a look a the spread.
What are you drawn to, where do your eyes want
to go...trust this. Often it is the most important thing,
or the root of the reading.

While taking your first look notice if the cards are dark
or light. If there are many dark cards the person is going
through some trauma or upset. If everything is bright
and sunny, the overall outlook would correspond.

Another important factor to consider are the
cards that point. If a card is pointing at another,
they are definitely connected. The pointing cards
lead us down the road to completing the story.
See where they lead you.

If you are drawn to a particular card take a
moment to gaze upon it. What stands out to you?
Is it a flower, a building, the road? Whatever it
is, blurt it out! I can't tell you how many times
something has stood out to me and I took a
chance and said something. 9 out of 10 times it
has some significance to the client.

This is particularly true with the Rider Waite Deck. Although I no longer use it myself, this iconic deck is firmly planted in the collective unconscious. Two of the most accurate readers I've ever met used the Rider Waite deck. Both would see things changing and moving around in the cards. On one instance while reading for me, she asked if I had been attacked by bees, which did happen. When I asked her how she got that, she said that the fire shooting out of the Tower turning into bees.

The Rider Wait has a lot of intricate details to look at. You may see letters or shapes in bushes, trees, garments, really anywhere in the cards.

Now that you've got the general idea, let's move on to the particular cards, and how they may tie into one another in a reading.

RODS (WANDS)

The Suit of Rods is also sometimes called Wands.
I prefer Rods and so I will refer to them as such.
Rods are akin to fire in the zodiac. The Fire signs
include Leo, Aries, Sagittarius. Events may involve
people of those signs, or occur in those times.

The Rods promote action and growth. The growth
can occur in many areas of life and on many levels.
If you see a lot of rods in a reading you know things
are moving and happening, progress is being made.

Rods are physical and represent physical activity.
Exercise, sports, and sex all are represented by
the rods.

While it's true the rods represent growth, sometimes
growth is initiated through strife and discord. When
many rods appear in the spread, friction, rebellion,
or fighting may be the order of the day.

ACE of WANDS.

The seeds been planted, and starting to grow.
You're on the right path, so go with the flow.

Two of Rods

The Two of Rods is a wonderful card to see in the spread. It means you are on the right path and a clear and trouble free road awaits you. Many of our troubles in life come from being on the wrong path or trying to fit a square peg into a round hole. To be on the right path is a blessing indeed.

Something that has always stood out to me in this card is the fact that he has the world in his hand. To me that says you can have it all! The world is your oyster! Although the card is a two, which is a low number. This signifies you are only in the beginning phases of this endeavor. But you have the world in your hand, so there is no limit to how far you can go with this.

As with all cards that are facing in a direction, it is important to not what he is looking at. Whatever he is looking at, is what the future holds. If he is facing a negative card, I feel that is only a minor obstacle to overcome. For the Two of Rods is so positive that nothing can stand in the way of success.

REVERSE

The Two of Rods in reverse tells us that you are on the wrong path. In a relationship reading it can mean a partnership will not work out. The cards around will shed light on why this is so.

It looks like your ship is about to come in.
You've done all the work, it's your time to win.

Three of Rods

The Three of Rods indicates your ships are coming in. Success is upon you now. No longer some distant goal in the future, it is within your sights. You can now take a moment to breath and acknowledge what you've achieved.

More often than not the accomplishment is in the way of business and career. Often it pertains to someone who is starting their own business. After a period of struggle or uncertainty, you finally have reached some solid ground. Now you have the backing and wherewithal to move onto the next plateau.

The Three of Rods pertains to success it's true. How this success will be achieved can be found in the surrounding cards. If the Emperor is near, than a VIP will be instrumental. If the Nine of Pentacles is near, it is success in your own business. If surrounded by cards such as the Six of Swords, or Eight of Cups, or Four of Rods, then you may have to relocate.

REVERSE

In reverse the Three of Rods means you will not have success in your current endeavors. It is better not to put all your eggs in one basket, keep your options open.

The changes at home bring you delight.
The new situation just feels so right.

Four of Rods

The Four of Rods almost always means a change
in your home. It can be literally a move to a new
home. It can be changing or redecorating you
home. It can be changes initiated by people
moving in or out. In general this card indicates
changes for the positive. The new environment
is usually happy and more harmonious for you.

There's a lot going on in this card. Therefore the
Four of Rods is a good card to get lost in and let
impressions flow. The people on the card, the
squiggly lines in the flower area. Let your mind
go and see if you get any impressions.

The Four of Rods has strong romantic
implications. In a love reading it usually means
the change in the home environment is living
together. Surrounded by love cards like the
Ten of Cups, Two of Cups, or the Lovers it means
a serious commitment. With the Four of Cups a
marriage proposal, or engagement.

REVERSE

The Four of Rods is one of only a few cards that
I really don't read much differently in reverse.
It is still a positive change in your home
environment. Sometimes in reverse the change
may not be romantic, but more practical. The
end result is still positive and happier than
before.

Strife and struggle rule the day.
Competition is stiff, at work and at play.

Five of Rods

The Five of Rods is a card of struggle. Things are not going smoothly. There is much opposition to your plan. There's something to be said for "the path of least resistance." Going against the grain may prolong the struggle and lead to unhappiness.

Look to the surrounding cards to find where the struggle arises. Court cards can show people who may be the opposition, or who may champion you. The cards following the Five of Rods will show if the struggle is worth it. If followed by the Six of Rods you may be victorious in the end. It may be worth the struggle if followed by Judgment. In that case it could be part of your Karmic growth.

REVERSE

The Five of Rods is a card that is much better in the reverse. In reverse it indicates that the struggle is over. It can also indicate that any struggle will be minimal and opposition will die down quickly.

You are the winner, you did the best.
You're head and shoulders above all the rest.

Six of Rods

The Six of Rods is known as the victory card.
In any type of competition you come out the
winner. This card can cover a wide range.
In Career matters, if you are viewing for a position
that and other's are being considered as well.
The Six of Rods tells us that you will come out on
top.In sports it will indicate a win for your team.
The Six of Rods can refer to getting into the
school of your choice, scoring well on a test
for a student.

An important note on the Six of Rods is that it
represents *earned* recognition. The success and
adoration your are experiencing is not a quirk of
fate. It has come to you because you've earned
it. You've done the work to be the best, and you
deserve every bit of it.

Look to the surrounding cards to see where the
victory lies. If the Hierophant is nearby it may
have to do with school or higher education.
If surrounded by pentacles, the victory could
be a job, promotion, or landing a contract.

REVERSE
The Six of Rods in reverse means you don't get
the promotion, or job. You don't do well on the
test, or get into the school you wanted. Because
the Six of Rods deals with earned recognition it
can sometimes mean you were treated unfairly.
In love relationships the Six of Rods in reverse
indicates that you are not getting the respect
you deserve from your partner.

Frustration comes at you
from left and from right.
You fend off the masses
and you win the fight.

Seven of Rods

The Seven of Rods indicates struggle and opposition. You are fending off the opposition for now, but you can't keep it up for ever. When the Seven of Rods shows up friction is coming at you from every which way. No time to stop and catch your breath. You're on the defensive and that's all you have time to do. It's like trying to stop a sinking ship that keeps springing a leak. Just when you've got one hole plugged, another hole springs up.

The cards that follow the Seven of Rods will tell the tale. If followed by bright and happy cards, the situation is only temporary and life will get easier soon. If followed by swords and dark cards, chances are you won't be able to handle the pressure for long, and should get out now.

The Seven of Rods shows up often in our busy past paced lifestyles. Many of us try to be super human with our constant multitasking. Nobody's system can handle a constant level of stress. The Seven of Rods can tell us to slow down and eliminate some of the stress in our lives.

REVERSE

The Seven of Rods in reverse is a serious warning to slow down now. You are not able to handle all the pressures, and it could be your undoing.

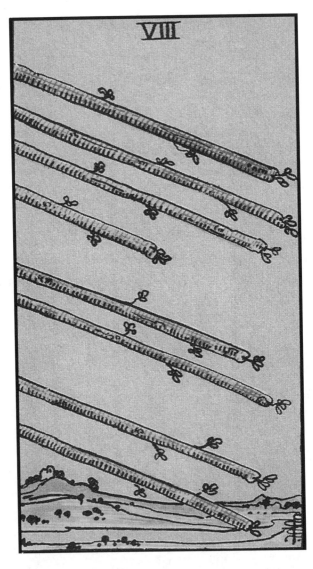

Things moving fast, news comes your way.
Don't hesitate, take action today.

Eight of Rods

The Eight of Rods means that news is on the way. It's Mercury and Uranus. In our modern time the Eight of Rods refers to all type of electronic media. Texting, Twittering, e-mails, and phone communications all fall under this card. What ever the case, it is happening fast, within days.

As with all pointing cards we look to see what it is pointing at. This will be very important in determining what is coming our way. If pointing at pentacles it can mean a check or electronic payment. If pointing at swords it can mean you could get some bad news soon. If pointing at the two of cups, it could mean a new love is on the way. If pointing at a court card, you will soon hear from that person.

REVERSE

The Eight of Rods in reverse means the news you were hoping for is not coming. In most cases it means not coming at all. In some cases it could mean a delay, or things are not moving as fast as you'd like.

You've got your guard up, defenses are high.
Hold down the fort 'til the storm passes by.

Nine of Rods

The Nine of Rods means that it is time to stand on your own. Be leery of who you talk to at this time and who you trust. Keep your plans to yourself, others may not have your best interest in mind. Now is not the time to wear your heart on your sleeve. Stand back and observe, get the lay of the land before you act.

The cards surrounding the Nine of Rods say a lot about what you need to be on guard about. I pay special attention to what the man is looking at. In the case of the Rider Waite, the card to the left.
If there is a court card there then that person is not to be trusted. If the Hierophant or Emperor is there it could be the Government. If the Hermit is there you are probably getting bad advise possibly from a lawyer or trusted advisor.

REVERSE

The Nine of Rods in reverse warns us that you are being too lax in your judgment. You need to be more discriminate in what you say and do.

A heavy burden is weighing you down.
It won't be forever, things turn around.

Ten of Rods

The Ten of Rods tells that that your are carrying a heavy load. You have hard work ahead of you, and it's not going to be easy. The bottom line is that you will accomplish your goal. It is not as noticeable in the Rider Waite as it is in the Hanson Roberts deck. But if you look close you can see that he is on the right path, and he is going to make it there.

The Ten of Rods is a card of burden you have taken on. Sometimes it can indicate that you are bearing all the responsibility while someone else gets a free ride. You are carrying the load for the both of you. The Ten of Rods can also relate to back problems in regards to health.

If the Ten of Rods is near any court cards in reverse you are carrying the load for someone else. If it falls around children cards like the Six of Cups, or the Sun, the person may be a single parent. And although they have a rough road to tow for the time being, it will be worth it in the long run.

REVERSE

The Ten of Rods in reverse is a welcome sign. It means the load is being lifted from your back at last. You feel the burden lifted. Your load is lightened and you can breath easy again.

SWORDS

The suit of swords represents upset, hurt, and all negative emotions. The swords are akin to air in the zodiac. The Air signs include: Aquarius, Libra, and Gemini. Events may involve people of those signs, or occur in those times.

The swords represent the traumas and disappointments in life. Anguish, heartache, and sorrow are represented in the swords.

If you see a lot of swords in the future cards, it is not too late to change your course. If in the present, be careful not to linger too long in depression. If in the past, the seeker has suffered great loss. Look to the present and future cards to find the road to recovery.

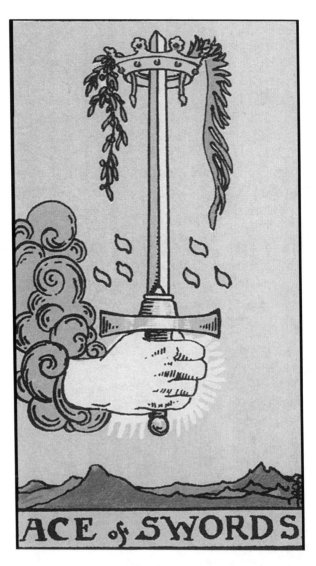

The sky's quite dark, and it looks pretty grim.
There still is a chance, hang in you can win.

Ace of Swords

The Ace of Swords is one of the few sword cards
that has some positive implications. It actually is
a card of victory. Even if the situation seems
hopeless and grim the Ace of Swords indicates
that there is still hope. From the darkness a crack
of light emerges. This is the first step in breaking
through the darkness into the light.

The Ace of Swords is definitely a victory and the
cards surrounding it will tell us how.
If the Ace of Swords comes after a lot of dark and
negative cards the Ace tells us the worst is over,
and a new day has dawned. If health is the
question the Ace of Swords can indicate the need
for surgery. It also tells us that the surgery will
be a success.

REVERSE

The Ace of Swords in reverse tells us that victory
is not possible at this time. It does not matter
how hard we work, or who we get on our side,
it is not happening. The opposing forces are too
strong and cannot be overcome at this time.

Six of these, or half dozen of another.
A decision must be made, one way or
the other.

Two of Swords

The Two of Swords in a reading tells us that there is a decision to be made. The trouble is it is all but impossible to decide. There is no clear cut answer in this case, you can't get a handle on it. You don't have all the information and you cannot see all sides of things.

Looking deeper into this card you can see there is water all around. Water is representative of emotions. Therefore the Two of Swords can be saying you are too emotionally involved to make an informed decision. If the moon is standing out to me, I may advise to wait until the moon changes signs for more clarity.

If you are the one awaiting the decision it tells us that the decision has not been made yet. The number two may play into the resolve, two days, two weeks. Again I would advise waiting until the moon changes sign to call or inquire.

REVERSE

The Two of Swords in reverse tells us that the decision has already been made. If it went in your favor or not can be told by the surrounding cards. If you are the one trying to decide, the Two of Swords in reverse tells us that you already know the answer, you just don't want to admit it. This is usually because the answer is not a popular one, but you must be true to yourself.

Your heart has been broke and you're
feeling blue.
You don't know what you're going to do.

Three of Swords

The Three of Swords is a card of heartbreak plain and simple. When the Three of Swords shows up in a reading there has been heartbreak and sorrow. If it shows in the future steps need to be taken now to change your path.

If the reading is about health the Three of Swords can warn us of heart trouble, or even a heart attack. If surrounded by a lot of stress cards like the Five of Rods, or Seven of Rods, it can be a forewarning of health problems to come.
You must immediately begin removing the stress from your life, or pay the consequences.

REVERSE

The Three of Swords in reverse does not change into a positive. Just as some of the more positive cards don't lose their power in reverse. The Three of Swords does not lose all of its power in reverse either. It does alleviate it somewhat. The pain may not be as bad as the upright, but is still there none the less.

Time for a healing, you need a rest.
Take some time out, then be at your best.

Four of Swords

The Four of Swords indicates a time for healing. After the trauma of the three of swords, it is now time to rest and regain your strength before moving forward. This seems to hold true in a reading. The person has been through a rough time, and a healing time is needed.

In our non stop society people don't want to slow down. It is necessary to relax in order to have a clear head. The Four of Swords is also an indicator to wait. Now is not the time to act. Wait for four days, or four months.

If the Four of Swords is accompanied by other health cards it is referring to an actual physical healing. If it is surrounded by rods, time to de-stress. If surrounded by pentacles, wait to act, don't buy or sell now.

REVERSE

The Four of Swords in reverse tells us it is time to get back into action. The healing time is over and you are ready to face the world again. If you have been waiting to take some sort of action in your life or if something's been on hold, now is the time to get back into it.

You can't win this one, you've hit a wall.
You're wasting your time going on with this
brawl.

Five of Swords

The Five of Swords is about wasting your energy. You may win the battle but you can never win the war. You've reached a stalemate and neither party is going to give in. They feel as strongly as you do and they are not budging.

To continue to try and press your point would be fruitless. This is a waste of energy on a grand scale. You are banging your head against the wall, and getting nowhere. Better to turn your attention elsewhere to make a difference.

The Five of swords accompanied by the Hierophant or Emperor says you are going up against the status quo. This is old school tradition, and they are not going to change or bend the rules.

REVERSE

The Five of Swords in reverse is a turn for the better. Compromises can be reached now. What once seemed important doesn't really matter now. You are ready to mend your fences.

You're moving forward with your life.
You've had enough of all the strife.

Six of Swords

The Six of Swords is a sign of change. You have had enough and are moving on. The rough waters are behind you, and calm waters lie ahead. You will have smooth sailing as you move toward you goals which are within sight.

The Six of Swords can also mean an actual journey. It can be a trip or vacation. It can also be a complete relocation. If the water is standing out I will say a journey by water, or by boat. Most of the time the journey is a journey of life, whether an actual physical move is involved or not.

Because the card shows movement and direction we want to take a look at the surrounding cards. What are they moving away from in the past? What are they moving forward to in the future?

REVERSE

The Six of Swords in reverse in movement stifled. Many times it involves an emotional blockage. The person may be unable to get over a hurtful or traumatic event. If a move or relocation is in question, the Six of Swords in reverse would tell us the trip will not happen.

Something's been taken away from you.
The question is, now what do you do?

Seven of Swords

If other people behave badly, and you do the same is that a victory? A victory on this level is an empty victory. You cannot control what other people do, but you can control how you react. It's not fulfilling to be right for the sake of being right. That is the way of the ego, not of the spirit.

Even if you do win, you have to ask yourself what you will lose in the process, Your dignity? Your friendships? Your self worth? Is anything really worth all that? To win at any cost is really of great cost.

If the Seven of Swords is accompanied by love cards such as the Two of Cups, or Lovers, this relationship will not be good for you, and you may lose yourself in the process. If the Seven of Swords shows up around the Two of Pentacles, or Five of Pentacles, you may lose your job, or your home.

REVERSE

The Seven of Swords in reverse is a turn for the better. Something is coming back to you that has been taken away. Self esteem, a job, a relationship, a sense of well being. You are on the way back.

You feel your trapped, there's no way out.
There is a way, just look about.

Eight of Swords

The Eight of Swords is a card of self imposed bondage. You've worked yourself into a state of fear and lack that you can't see clearly now. The figure is not completely surrounded there is a way out. They just refuse to see it. Usually because they are caught up in their own sorrow and worry.

You could think of each of those swords as an excuse as to why you are not living up to your true potential. "What I would really love to be doing is...but I can't because..." With every "because" you add another sword. Every sword is another bar in a cage of your own making. The figure has a blindfold on which shows me they are so in their head. They only need open their eyes, or remove the blindfold to see the freedom that awaits.

REVERSE

The Eight of Swords in reverse is all about freedom. Freedom from false fears, stress, and worries that can block us from living our truest life.

No one sees a tear you shed.
You cry at night alone in bed.

Nine of Swords

The Nine of Swords is a card of sorrow. It is a card of overwhelming grief. Often the person is trying to put on a brave face, and keep up a good front. When in reality they are suffering more than anyone knows. This grief is not unfounded. There is a legitimate hurt that's not easily gotten over.

Another manifestation of the Nine of Swords is incessant worrying. The kind of worrying that keeps you up nights. Accompanied by pentacles you could be worried about your job or finances. With the Empress it could be health related.

REVERSE

The Nine of Rods in reverse isn't much better. It is still a card of great grief. The severity may be less, but it still hurts. Sometimes it can be not as bad, because you saw it coming and had some time to prepare.

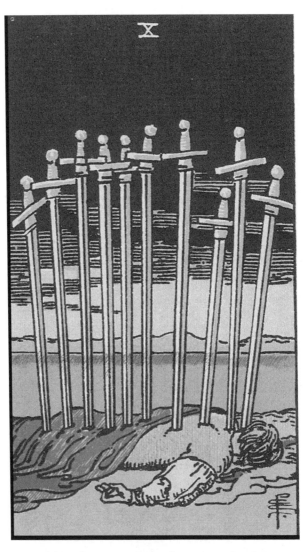

The devastation that you feel,
Is going to take some time to heal.

Ten of Swords

The Ten of Swords is a card of total ruin.
Just as aces are new beginnings, tens are the
culmination, the most, if you will. As swords
represent pain and suffering, the Ten of Swords
is the most pain, and the most suffering. It is
sometimes rightfully known as the worst card
in the deck.

How deep the wounds, and how long it takes to
heal will depend on the cards surrounding it.
If surrounded by other swords and dark cards, the
wounds may be very deep indeed. If surrounded
by bright cards such as the Sun, or the Ace of
Cups, then the worst is over and things should
improve soon.

REVERSE

In reverse the Ten of Swords is really not much
better. It is one of those cards that is so powerful
that its meaning does not change much in reverse.
It only lessens the blow to some extent.

CUPS

Cups are all about love, creativity, emotions, relationships. Cups are akin to the element of water in the zodiac. The water signs include Cancer, Scorpio, Pisces. Events may involve people of those signs, or occur in those times.

The suit of cups is the equivalent to the hearts in a regular deck of playing cards. Therefore the cups relate strongly to matters of the heart. Marriage, love, and children are all represented in the cups.

A reading with a lot of cups reveals that emotions are involved. If the cards are bright, in it foretells of much happiness and joy. If dark, it may show sorrow and depression.

ACE of CUPS.

A new beginning is in store for you.
It may involve love, or creativity too.

Ace of Cups

The Ace of Cups is the beginning of all things good. Most of the time it is thought of as a new beginning in love. With it brings that exhilarating feeling you get when falling in love. Everything is beautiful and you see the world through rose colored glasses. A new romantic relationship is the most common meaning. But it can also refer to a friendship with someone you are going to hit it off with.

The Ace of Cups can also represent a new beginning in creativity. Your cup is overflowing with creative ideas. You can barely get them down fast enough. You have a great sense of well being because the energy of spirit is flowing through you.

The Ace of Cups can also mean a spiritual awakening, or setting out upon the spiritual path. If the Ace of Cups is accompanied other love cards then we are looking at a relationship. If the Empress is near by, it could be a pregnancy. If surrounded by pentacles, you will be starting a job you love in which you will have a lot of creative input.

REVERSE

The Ace of Cups in reverse tells us that the cup has run dry. A relationship has lost its sparkle. In the future a relationship will not get off the ground. The creative project is abandoned.

A kindred spirit has entered your life.
You may end up as husband and wife.

Two of Cups

The Two of Cups is known as "the soul mate card."
When this card shows up you know love is in the air.
This is someone with who you see eye to eye.
You are connected in a way that can only be
explained by love.

The majority of the time, we are dealing with a
romantic relationship. Although this card can show
up in just about any context. Just as we encounter
kindred spirits in all walks of life. It can be
a child, family member, coworker, or even a
complete stranger. "Soul mates" come into our
lives under many guises.

If the Two of Cups shows with other love cards
we are looking at romantic love. With Judgment-
a deeply karmic relationship. With the Sun or Six
of Cups - a child. Look to the court cards nearby
to see who this soul mate is.

REVERSE

The Two of Cups in reverse usually mean a break
up, or falling out. Just because someone is a soul
mate does not mean you will live happily ever
after. Souls come into our lives for many different
reasons. Look to the other cards in the spread for
more insights.

A time of great joy, and much celebration.
Weddings and Holidays, accept invitations.

Three of Cups

The Three of Cups tells us that happy times are upon us. For me personally the Three of Cups is me and my two daughters. It can be any group celebration and often does involve women. This card tells us that good times await and to get out and socialize.

You can use the Three of Cups as a timing card because is represents holidays and celebrations. If you are looking for a timer, look to the next holiday. If you have a wedding or reunion coming up, the timing of that event could factor in.

The other cards in the spread will tell you more about the situation. If the Empress is nearby it is probably a baby shower. Next to the Ten of Cups, a wedding shower. Near the Hierophant a class reunion. Lots of Pentacles a work related function.

REVERSE

The Three of Cups in reverse usually indicates someone has been partying too much. If near the Moon in reverse it can show an addiction to drugs or alcohol. Near the Hermit or Four of Swords - you need to get out more and socialize.

An offering has come your way.
It's up to you, is it yea or it nay?

Four of Cups

The Four of Cups is an offer coming your way.
You are hesitant, and not sure if you want to
accept. The cards to the left will show us where
the offer is coming from. While the cards to the
right show what the offer will yield if accepted.

If the Four of Cups is near the Lovers, or Ten of
Cups, or Four of Rods, it can indicate a marriage
proposal. If surrounded by pentacles it could be
a job offer. If Justice is nearby it can dealing with
an offer toward settling a legal matter. If near
the Ten of pentacles and Four of Rods, it may
have to do with a real estate transaction.
If followed by the Devil or Tower, you would
be better off turning the offer down.

REVERSE

The Four of Cups in reverse is an offer you can't
refuse. You don't have to stop and think about it,
it's what you've been waiting to hear and you
jump on it without hesitation.

Look to the future, the past is behind.
The cloud over head, may be silver lined.

Five of Cups

The Five of Cups is a case of crying over spilled milk...literally. The figure is looking back in sorrow at what they have lost. Their main area of focus is on what went wrong and what they lost. The Five of Cups is a card of disappointment and sorrow. Chances are you are dealing with someone who is depressed.

An important thing to keep in mind with the Five of Cups is that all the cups have not spilled. There are still full cups available. The figure cannot see them because they are so focused on what has gone wrong. One only has to focus on what is good, and everything will start to change.

If there are many swords in the spread this person may have suffered a serious trauma. A death of a loved one is a distinct possibility. If the Six of Cups is near, they may be longing for their youth or days gone by. If the Ten of Cups in reverse is in the spread, the person has not been able to move on from a divorce or break up.

REVERSE

The Five of Cups in reverse is a sign of a healing and moving forward with your live. You are tired of feeling bad about the past, and are ready to look into the future.

A friend from the past has come back around.
The good times await, and joy can be found.

SIx of Cups

The Six of Cups nearly always has connections to
the past. Usually a person from your past is
coming back into your life. The level of
involvement depends on the surrounding cards.
It could be anything from running into someone
and doing a quick catch up. Or maybe rekindling
a former romance.

The Six of Cups can also be a reference to a past
happiness or state of mind, and not necessarily
involve another person at all. The Six of Cups is
often a reference to your childhood. Where you
lived, pets you had, what you wanted to be when
you grew up, what you were studying to be.

The Six of Cups can represent actual children in
your life. Cards to look for would be The Sun, or
any Pages in the spread. If the Six of Cups is near
The Lovers, or Two of Cups, a romance is being
rekindled. If surrounded by pentacles, you may
be going back to an old job, or a field you used
to work in. It could also indicate a friend from
the past could help you in your career.

REVERSE

The Six of Cups in reverse tells us to release the past
If you are hoping to get back together with someone,
it is unlikely that it will happen.

Visualize your hearts desire.
Make it happen, then aim higher.

Seven of Cups

The Seven of Cups is all about visualization. Creative visualization is a powerful tool for manifesting your life's direction. If you can see it in your mind, then it can be a reality. Visualize what you want to achieve with the greatest detail you can muster. This will bring you closer to your heart's desire.

If you are creative or in the arts, The Seven of Cups can bring much inspiration. If you are able to see it in you minds eye, hear it with your hearts ear, that is the first step in creation.

The Seven of Cups can also indicate the awakening of psychic abilities. Developing clairvoyance is a definite possibility.
This would be true if The Star is nearby.

REVERSE

In reverse The Seven of Cups tells us that you are starting to see results. You dreams are becoming a reality. You start getting confirmation.

Cut your losses, walk away.
You'll live to fight another day.

Elght of Cups

The Eight of Cups is one of the journey cards.
It can be an actual journey, but often it is an
emotional journey, or a journey of spirit.
After all we are dealing with the Cups. Take note
of all the cups stacked up. It took time to stack
all those cups. This is something you have vested
a lot of time and energy into. Never the less,
it is time to move on and don't look back.

The Eight of Cups often does refer to an actual
journey. If other journey cards are around like
The Chariot, or The Six of Swords a physical
journey is likely. The water element could
come into play. The trip could be near water.
Sometimes it refers to a boat trip or cruise.

The Eight of Cups can be used as a timing card.
Look at the moon, if the full moon stands out to
you, then the full moon is the timing factor.
If the crescent moon stands out, then it may
be the new moon. Also consider quarter moons.

REVERSE

The Eight of Cups in reverse shows a reluctancy
to move on from the past. It doesn't matter any
more how much time or effort you've put into it.
It is time to cut your losses and move on.

A wish coming true, a hope, a dream.
The glow of health within you beams.

Nine of Cups

The Nine of Cups is known as "the Wish Card." This is one of the best cards in the deck, your wish is coming true. The figure on the card is well fed and has excess stored up to last him through the winter. Being well fed was once a sign of wealth. Having plenty to eat, and not doing any hard labor will result in a few extra pounds.

The Nine of Cups is a sign of great health and robust. If there is any health concerns, you can expect a full recovery with the Nine of Cups. This is especially true if The Sun, or The Empress is near by.

The Nine of Cups is a card of the physical world. If the Ace of Pentacles is near, you'll get the new job. With the Six of Pentacles, you get a raise or a loan. Your wish is definitely coming true, the other cards will tell if it turns out how you hoped.

REVERSE

The Nine of Cups in Reverse is simply that your wish is not coming true. The Nine of Cups more often refers to the smaller things in life, and not the big picture.

A happier time there could not be.
Marriage is a big possibility.

Ten of Cups

The Ten of Cups is commonly known as the marriage card. In a reading it almost always refers to a marriage or a serious committed relationship. It is important to note the children in the card. If they are standing out to me I will predict children from the union. If it is a second marriage it shows me that the kids all get along with each other, and with the new step parent.

Just as aces are new beginnings, tens are the culmination. So the Ten of Cups is the most happiness, the most love, the most joy that a soul can experience. If the couple stands out to me, it's about a relationship. Sometimes if the cups stand out to me, it may be joy and celebration.

If the Ten of Cups is with the Two of Cups or Judgment, the people have been together for many life times and will finally be fulfilled in this incarnation. If with The Six of Cups, or Sun the emphasis may be around children and family love.

REVERSE

The Ten of Cups in reverse indicates a break up or divorce. Where it is in the spread will indicate if it has already occurred, or is yet to come.

PENTACLES

The pentacles are related to money, finance, and the material world. The pentacles are akin to the element of earth in the tarot. The earth signs include Taurus, Capricorn, and Virgo. Events may involve people of those signs, or occur in those times.

If there is an abundance of pentacles in the spread you are dealing with money, career, finance, real estate, brick and mortar buildings, possesions, things crafted.

When court cards are surrounded in pentacles, you may be dealing with someone who is involved in the financial arena. Bankers, brokers, and investors would fall under this category.

A new beginning in money is on the way.
A job or a business is likely to pay.

Ace of Pentacles

The Ace of Pentacles is a new beginning in money. The most common meaning is a new job. It can also be a raise. If you have your own business it can be a new client, or project you are about to begin.

The Ace of Pentacles is a positive omen in a reading. Your income is about to increase. It indicates that the new project or business that you are starting is going to produce an income. Move forward with your plans. This is also a good card to do some scrying on. Look at the plants on the fence in the background. What stands out? The flowers? The mountains?

The other cards in the spread will give you more details. If near the Ten of Pentacles, or the World, this thing will be bigger than you can even imagine. If there is a lot of cups, you love what you do and the money is not a factor.

REVERSE

The Ace of Pentacles in reverse tells us that the new beginning you are hoping for is not likely to happen. You don't get the job, the business never gets off the ground.

Money comes in, and it goes back out.
Finances are rocky without a doubt.

Two of Pentacles

The Two of Pentacles is a card of financial turbulence. You are juggling your finances, robbing Peter to pay Paul. The water in the background shows turbulence, you are struggling to make it. As of now, you are handling it.

Sometimes the Two of Pentacles can indicate you are working a second job to get ahead. If you are a freelancer, you may have two projects going on at the same time. If you are a musician you may be playing with more than one group.

If the Two of Pentacles is near the Seven of Rods or the Ten of Rods, you are struggling indeed. The cards that follow will show how you handle the pressure. If followed by a lot of dark cards and swords, you cannot keep it up. If followed by the Sun and other bright cards, things will improve, your work will pay off. If followed by the Empress in reverse, your health could suffer.

REVERSE

The Two of Pentacles in reverse tells us that your struggles are waning. Finances are becoming more manageable.

You've crafted a thing of great renowned.
Many admirers gather around.

Three of Pentacles

The Three of Pentacles represents something that you have created. You reveal your work and others are impressed. Because it is a pentacle card, money is involved. You may get a commission or grant. You may be offered a job based on your talent and previous work.

Sometimes when I look at the card it represents school, especially college. It can be a card of mastering your craft as an apprentice as were. Most of the time in modern days it would imply higher more specialized education. If the hammer and chisel stands out to me it can mean a job in the trades, working with your hands.

If the Three of Pentacles is near the Hierophant we are talking about college. If it is near the Sun, it will usually refer to someone in the arts. Next to the World, it tells us that what you are building now will far surpass your expectations.

REVERSE

The Three of Pentacles in reverse indicates that you need more experience or study. You are not ready to reveal your project yet, it needs more work.

Don't hold too tight, give it some room.
Being a miser leads only to gloom.

Four of Pentacles

The Four of Pentacles is the miser card. If you hold on to your money and possessions too tight, it becomes stagnant. Money must circulate in order to come back to you. Loosen your belt a little and let the prosperity energy flow.

Often when someone is stingy with money, they are stingy with affection and praise as well. The Four of Pentacles can represent someone who is cold and petty. This type of person is just looking for what they can get out of you, and give nothing in return.

The Four of Pentacles can also represent a hoarder. Someone who hangs on to possessions to the point of it all turn to junk. If you hold on too tight to anything, it destroys it. If this card shows near a court card in a relationship reading this person is cold and stingy.

REVERSE

The Four of Pentacles in reverse can show someone who is finally loosening up and becoming more giving. If the Fool in reverse is nearby it can indicate that someone blows every penny they get and can't save a dime.

It seem like things are going wrong.
Keep your chin up, try to stay strong.

Five of Pentacles

The Five of Pentacles is the poverty consciousness card. The people in the card are clearly down and out. Even though there are pentacles to be had, they walk right by apparently oblivious to them. We have to believe we deserve prosperity before it can manifest in our life.

The poverty consciousness can manifest in others ways besides our finances. Ill health is another manifestation of the poverty or victim consciousness. If you are the victim, then you don't have to take responsibility for the state you find yourself in. It's somebody else's fault.

If the Five of Pentacles is near the Empress in reverse it is an indication of ill health. If it shows up near the Devil the person has deep seated beliefs that won't be easily broken. If near the Lovers in reverse, they feel they are not good enough for their partner.

REVERSE

The Five of Cups in reverse indicates you are coming out of a bad spell. Your self esteem is on the rise and you're starting to feel like your old self again.

You receive a financial reward.
A raise or a loan, your credit restored.

Six of Pentacles

The Six of Pentacles is a card of financial rewards. It does not represent a windfall, this is earned income. You earned it from previous performance. Most often it indicates a raise or promotion in work.

If you have applied for a grant the Six of Pentacles says you will get it. The same would hold true if you were applying for a loan. The number six can also come into play as a timing element. Six days, six months, the sixth day, the sixth month, etc.

If the Six of Pentacles shows up near the Ten of Pentacles, we are talking about a large sum of money indeed. If it shows near Justice, it can mean a reward from a lawsuit. Near the Empress and Six of Cups, we could be talking about child support.

REVERSE

The Six of Pentacles in reverse tells us you will not receive the raise, or get the grant or reward. Sometimes the Six of Pentacles in reverse simply means you are not being paid what you're worth.

You've worked very hard and deserve
time to rest.
You've achieved some success, now
what to do next.

Seven of Pentacles

The Seven of Pentacles indicates you've been working hard and amassed some cash. You have a little time to take a breather and decide what to do next. This is one of those cards can mean different things depending on how it looks to me.

If the guys face looks stressful it will mean that you worry about money all the time. Or it can say you are a workaholic. If the Money stands out the Seven of Pentacles shows me of a large sum, or pile of money bestowed upon you in a one time payment.

If the Seven of Pentacles shows up next to the Wheel of Fortune, a windfall is likely. If it shows up near the Five of Rods you earned the money through your own toiling. If it shows up near Justice, you may receive an annuity or monetary award.

REVERSE

If the Seven of Pentacles is in reverse you are not overly focused on finances at this time. The other cards in the spread will tell were your attention lies. With the Eight of Swords - you worry too much.

You love what you do, and would do it for free.
The fact that they pay you, fills you with glee.

Eight of Pentacles

The Eight of Pentacles is the card of the craftsman. He loves what he's doing and even though he is accumulating pentacles (money), he doesn't seem to notice. He is totally into what he is doing. He loves what he does and the money comes easily.

The Eight of Pentacles tells us you are on the right path. Finding your right vocation is a great gift in life. When you've found your path you want to do it all the time whether you get paid or not. Make no mistake with the Eight of Pentacles you are getting paid, and paid well.

If the Eight of Pentacles is near the Judgment card you are implementing skills that you've acquired over many lifetimes. If it is near the Emperor, you may be blessed with a powerful benefactor.

REVERSE

The Eight of Pentacles in reverse tells us that you hate your job basically. You get no personal satisfaction, and do it only for money. Your job is draining your energy and making you miserable.

Your business is booming
you're on top of the heap.
The rewards of success it is now time to reap.

Nine of Pentacles

The Nine of Pentacles is a card of financial success. Your finances are under control so you now have time to turn your attention to the finer things in life. If the bird stands out, you love your pets, or may be adopting a new one. If the castle in the background stands out, you may be fixing up your house. If the garden plants show up, you may be a master gardener.

When the Nine of Pentacles shows up it often implies the person has their own business. The business is flourishing and they now have more free time. Again much depends on what is standing out on the card. If her dress stands out, they may be in the clothing business, or a designer. If the castle stands out, it could be real estate. If the plants stand out, they may be a landscape designer.

If the Nine of Pentacles shows up near the World, you will have success beyond your wildest dreams. If it shows up near the High Priestess, you use your intuition to guide your business decisions.

REVERSE

The Nine of Pentacles in reverse is a sign of financial distress. Your business is on life support, you are not as self sufficient as you once were.

Your profits are becoming healthy.
You're on your way to being wealthy.

Ten of Pentacles

The Ten of Pentacles is known as the big money card. As with all tens it is the culmination. The Ten of Pentacles is the most money, the most wealth, the most success. There's a lot to look at, and the images that stand out can mean different things.

If the elderly man stands out, the Ten of Pentacles can foretell an inheritance. If the buildings stand out it can be related to real estate. If the man and woman stand out, you may be marrying into a wealthy family. If the dogs stand out, it can mean you pamper your pets.

If the Ten of Pentacles shows up near the Four of Wands you may do well on a real estate deal.
If it is near the Ace of Pentacles and Six of Wands, you beat out the competition for a high paying position.

REVERSE

The Ten of Pentacles in reverse indicates loss. You are living beyond your means and need to cut back on unnecessary expenses.

COURT CARDS

The court cards are for the most part people. Queens are women, Kings and Knights are men. Many say pages are young boys or girl. I rarely use pages as people at all. I consider pages messengers.

I also use the Pages and all of the court cards as timers. If there is a Pentacle court card, ie King, Queen, Knight, or Page of Pentacles, then we are looking at the time of an earth sign. So that would be in the time Taurus, Capricorn, or Virgo. I always go to the next available sign. For instance if it is March I would say this event is occurring in the time of Taurus. Taurus being the next earth sign coming up after March. If it is the Swords, we are looking at air sign timing. Cups is the water signs, and Rods are fire. I have found this method to be very accurate for me.

Sometimes it can refer to the moon sign which changes every couple of days. I use the moon method when you know an event is happening in a shorter window of time, and is not months away. For example say a woman is at full term pregnancy and she wants to know the date. You get a pentacle court card. So you look for the next earth sign moon, and that is your date.

Speaking of pregnant women, I also use the court cards to predict the sex of the baby as well.
I have the mother to be cut the cards if I am reading her in person. Or I will have her tell me when to stop shuffling if over the phone. I do no spread at all, I simply start flipping the cards and the first court card to show will predict the sex. For instance if I get the knight of pentacles, I say boy, the queen would be a girl.

If you get no court card within the first 10 cards, then the accuracy goes down. If a court card comes up in the first three cards, then it is usually very accurate.

As with all cards with people on them, take a minute to look at the face. How do they seem to you? Happy, sad, angry, frustrated, etc. This is one of those things you should blurt out, as it often pertains to the reading.

The Astrology used for the timing is also true for the sun signs of people involved. Below is a run down of the elements.

Rods = Fire = Aries, Leo, Sagittarius

Swords = Air = Aquarius, Gemini, Pisces

Pentacles = Earth = Taurus, Capricorn, Virgo

Cups = Water = Scorpio, Cancer, Pisces

PAGES

Traditionally Pages are considered children of either sex. However, as I said earlier I almost never use them as people. Rather I use them as messengers. Their element will tell us the time.

PAGE of WANDS.

News comes of fun and excitement.
You want to join in, you don't need
much enticement.

Page of Rods

The news you have been waiting for is coming in
the time of the next fire sign. The news may require
you to act quickly, or the opportunity might slip
away. The Page of Rods can be related to entertainment,
sports, or blazing a new trail.

REVERSE

The Page of Rods in reverse says the news is not
coming, or it will not be the news you want to
hear. When the Page of Rods is in reverse, it is
not time to act, wait for more favorable conditions.

PAGE of SWORDS.

Phone calls and emails bring you the news.
An air sign could want to tell you their views.

Page of Swords

The news you have been waiting for is coming in
the time of the next air sign. It could also pertain
to news regarding travel, the internet, moving.
The Page of swords is akin to Mercury, speaking,
writing, and all forms of communication are favored.

REVERSE

The Page of Swords in reverse says the news is not
coming, or it will not be the news you want to hear.
You may be suffering from writer's block. It may
be hard to find the right words to express yourself.

PAGE of CUPS.

News is coming any day.
Remember your dreams, it could just pay.

Page of Cups

The news you have been waiting for is coming in the time of the next water sign. It could also pertain to news regarding love and emotions. Sometimes the Page of Cups can be a marriage proposal.

REVERSE

The Page of Cups in reverse says the news is not coming, or it will not be the news you want to hear. A love interest may not return your affections.

PAGE of PENTACLES

News of money is coming your way.
It's what you've been wanting, you're going
to get paid.

Page of Pentacles

The news you have been waiting for is coming in
the time of the next earth sign. The news could
pertain to money or job, real estate or property.

REVERSE

The Page of Pentacles in reverse says the news is
not coming, or it will not be the news you want
to hear. A financial backer may withdraw, or a
job offer is not what it seems.

KNIGHTS

Knights are young men. Their element represents their astrological sign. Sometimes the sun sign won't match, but you'll recognize the person by the qualities they represent.

I no longer assign a specific age cut off between Knights and Kings. What's older to me, may not be to someone else. So now I just say an older or younger man relative to the age of the client.

Some times age is completely irrelevant. In this case Knights and Kings are determined by level of maturity rather than age.

KNIGHT of WANDS.

Medium complexion with red in his hair.
A younger fire sign man, has quite the flair.

Knight of Rods

The Knight of Rods can be a fire sign, or have reddish hair, or both. I've noticed with the Knight of Rods that the red hair may be in his facial hair more than on his head.
The Knight of Rods is Mr. excitement. He's fun to be around. In a romance he's not shy, and it is not uncommon for him to court you with grand gestures. He'll shout his love from the roof tops and make you feel exhilarated.

REVERSE

In reverse the Knight of Rods is having a negative effect on your life, or standing in your way. Look to the spread to see what he is standing in the way of you obtaining. The Knight of Rods in reverse can be selfish and childish.

KNIGHT of SWORDS .

Hazel brown eyes and medium hair.
He brings you the news, his element air.

Knight of Swords

The Knight of Swords in a young man who may be an Air sign, or medium complected, or both. The Knight of Swords is a talker, he is eloquent and well spoken. He has a quick wit and can make you laugh. In a relationship he may write you love letters or poems.

REVERSE

In reverse the Knight of Swords is having a negative effect on your life, or standing in your way.
Look to the spread to see what he is standing in the way of you obtaining. The Knight of Swords in reverse can be mean and insulting. He may act superior and try and talk over others.

KNIGHT of CUPS.

Golden hair, and eyes of blue.
A younger man brings love to you.

Knight of Cups

The Knight of Cups is a young man who may be a water sign, light complected, or both. The Knight of Cups is a romantic. He carries the cup of love extended outward. He wears his heart on his sleeve. He is artistic and sensitive.

REVERSE

In reverse the Knight of Cups is having a negative effect on your life, or standing in your way. Look to the spread to see what he is standing in the way of obtaining. The Knight of Cups in reverse may have a drinking or drug problem.

KNIGHT of PENTACLES.

He's earthy and true, his complexion is dark.
This younger man is in business, a shark.

Knight of Pentacles

The Knight of Pentacles is a young man who is an earth sign, dark complected, or both. He is practical and hard working. In a relationship he is slow to show his feelings. Once committed he is true blue faithful.

REVERSE

In reverse the Knight of Pentacles is having a negative effect on your life, or standing in your way.
Look to the spread to see what he is standing in the way of you obtaining. The Knight of Pentacles in reverse can be cold and aloof. He also could be a workaholic.

QUEENS

The Queens represent women. Their element represents their astrological sign. Sometimes the sun sign won't match, but you'll recognize the person by the qualities they represent.

QUEEN of WANDS.

Medium complexion with red in her hair.
This fiery red head, has quite the flair.

Queen of Rods

The Queen of Rods is a fire sign, a red head, or both. It's funny to note how many fire sign ladies dye their hair red, even if they're not a natural red head. The Queen a Rods is a dynamo. She's motivated driven, and is great fun to be around.

REVERSE

In reverse the Queen of Rods is having a negative effect on your life, or standing in your way. Look to the spread to see what he is standing in the way of you obtaining. The Queen of Rods in reverse can be pushy and obnoxious.

QUEEN of SWORDS.

Hazel brown eyes, and medium hair.
She brings you the news, her element air.

Queen of Swords

The Queen of Swords is an air sign, medium complected, or both. The Queen a Swords is very verbal, she never runs out of things to say. She's intelligent, charming, and witty.

REVERSE

In reverse the Queen of Swords is having a negative effect on your life, or standing in your way.
Look to the spread to see what he is standing in the way of you obtaining. The Queen of Swords in reverse can be catty or a gossip.

QUEEN of CUPS.

Golden hair, and eyes of blue.
An intuitive woman brings love to you.

Queen of Cups

The Queen of Cups is a water sign, a blonde, or both. It's funny to note how many water sign ladies dye their hair blonde, even if they're not a natural blonde. The Queen a Cups is warm and caring. She is creative, nurturing, and artistic.

REVERSE

In reverse the Queen of Cups is having a negative effect on your life, or standing in your way. Look to the spread to see what he is standing in the way of you obtaining. The Queen of Cups in reverse can be an alcoholic or drug addict. She may also suffer from depression.

QUEEN of PENTACLES

She's earthy and true, he's complexion is dark.
This savvy woman is in business, a shark.

Queen of Pentacles

The Queen of Pentacles is an earth sign, or dark complected, or both. The Queen a Pentacles is a career girl. She's capable and reliable. She likes the finer things in life, and doesn't mind working for them.

REVERSE

In reverse the Queen of Pentacles is having a negative effect on your life, or standing in your way. Look to the spread to see what he is standing in the way of you obtaining. The Queen of Pentacles in reverse can be cool and calculating.

KINGS

Kings are older men. As stated above what's old or young is relative to your age. So I stopped assigning a specific cut off between Knights and Kings. Also I noticed that sometimes age has nothing to do with it. A man young in years can be more mature than a man older in years.

KING of WANDS

Medium complexion with red in his hair.
An older fire sign man, has quite the flair.

King of Rods

The King of Rods is a fire sign, a red head, or both. As with the Knight, I've noticed with the King of Rods that the red hair may be in his facial hair more than on his head.

The King of Rods is also exciting. He has a twinkle in his eye that crackles like fire. He'll whisk you away on whim. He is romantic and knows how to court a lady.

REVERSE

In reverse the King of Rods is having a negative effect on your life, or standing in your way. Look to the spread to see what he is standing in the way of you obtaining. The King of Rods in reverse can also be selfish and childish.

KING of SWORDS.

Hazel brown eyes, and medium hair.
He brings you the news, his element air.

King of Swords

The King of Swords in a mature man who may be an Air sign, or medium complected, or both. Often the King of Swords will have gray or salt and pepper hair. He is well read, and well traveled. He has accumulated much knowledge in his time on earth. He is witty and charming and stimulating to be around.

REVERSE

In reverse the King of Swords is having a negative effect on your life, or standing in your way. Look to the spread to see what he is standing in the way of you obtaining. The King of Swords in reverse can have a biting tongue, and feel he is intellectually superior to everyone.

KING of CUPS.

Golden hair, and eyes of blue.
An older man brings love to you.

King of Cups

The King of Cups is a mature man who may be a water sign, light complected, or both. The King of Cups is a mystic. He sees into the souls of people, but often keeps it to himself. He is romantic and creative.

REVERSE

In reverse the King of Cups is having a negative effect on your life, or standing in your way. Look to the spread to see what he is standing in the way of obtaining. The King of Cups in reverse may have a drinking or drug problem.

KING of PENTACLES.

He's earthy and true, his complexion is dark.
This older man is in business, a shark.

King of Pentacles

The King of Pentacles is a mature man who is an earth sign, dark complected, or both. He is a land owner. He is the boss at work, or owns the company. He is successful and enjoys the finer things in life.

REVERSE

In reverse the Knight of Pentacles is having a negative effect on your life, or standing in your way.
Look to the spread to see what he is standing in the way of you obtaining. In reverse the King of Pentacles can try to buy and sell people.

MAJOR ARCANA

The Major Arcana or Trump cards are above our earthly toilings. There is more to this life than our ego driven agendas. The Major Arcana represent the bigger reasons we're here. The lessons we chose to learn in this incarnation. If there are many Major Arcana cards in the spread, there are higher forces at work.

THE FOOL.

Take a leap, don't sit and ponder.
Life's awaiting you out yonder.

The Fool

The Fool's Number is Zero. He's fresh and new like a new born babe. He has complete trust in the Universe. He knows that if he takes that step, something will be there to land on.

The Fool is open and free. He has no hang ups or worries. The Fool is all about having faith. You're at the beginning of a new path. No one can ever say for sure where it will lead. But if you don't take that first step, you'll never know. Have the courage to blaze a new trail in the direction of your heart's true desire.

You can see where the Fool's path leads by the other cards in the spread. It is also important to note what is behind him, for that is what is being left behind. If the Fool is walking toward Pentacles, a new career path is in store. With Cups a new relationship.

REVERSE

The Fool in reverse say that you are making the same mistake over and over. Your attempted new beginnings are really the same drama playing out over and over again. Learn the lesson so you can move on.

THE MAGICIAN.

Moving forward with your plan.
All you need is close at hand.

The Magician

The Magician is a powerful symbol of self realization. He is well equipped to handle any situation.
He has conquered all four of the elements and can utilize them at will. He is driven and ready for action. The infinity symbol over is head tells us that there is no limit to how far you can go.

As with all pointing cards it is important to look at what the Magician is pointing at in the spread. Even in the reverse position, it is important to note what he's pointing out to you.

Because the Magician is so resourceful and that he stands alone, he will often represent having your own business. This is especially true if it is near the Nine of Pentacles. If the Magician is near the Four of Swords, you're rested and ready to get back into action.

REVERSE

The Magician in reverse can be an indication of an abuse of power. More often it can mean you are trying to fit a square peg into a round hole. No matter how hard you push it is just not going to happen. Save your energy.

THE HIGH PRIESTESS

Let intuition be your guide.
You know the answer deep inside.

The High Priestess

The High Priestess is two, the feminine, the
mystery, the psychic, the seer, the goddess.
She is all of that and more. She represents
the power of feminine energy. In a man's reading
she is his ideal woman.

The High Priestess is the card of the psychic.
You may have psychic ability. Or if there is a queen
near by, she may be the psychic. Whether you
believe you are "psychic" or not, when the High
Priestess is in the reading you should trust your
intuition. Spirit is trying to communicate with
you...listen.

If the High Priestess is near the Moon, we are
definitely talking about psychic ability. With the
Moon it may be tied to your dreams. Start a
dream journal. You may get insights or see that
you are having precognitive dreams.

REVERSE

The High Priestess in reverse is a woman who is
deceptive. She is hiding behind the veil of
illusion. She cannot be trusted, she has ulterior
motives.

THE EMPRESS.

Harvest, comfort, health is fine.
Someone's pregnant at this time.

The Empress

The Empress is known as the pregnancy card.
She is brimming with abundance. She is the mother,
she is motherhood. If the Empress does not
represent a pregnancy, then it is likely that she
is your mother.

The Empress is also a fantastic health card.
She is the picture of health. If there are any health
concerns at the time of the reading, and the
Empress shows up, all will be well. She is
particularly relevant to women's health issues.

If the Empress is near the Sun, we are definitely
talking about a pregnancy. If the Six of Cups is in
the spread, there is more than one child. This
configuration could also indicate a multiple birth,
twins etc. The Empress with the Three of
Pentacles, your artistic endeavors will flourish.

REVERSE

The number one interpretation of the Empress
in reverse is an abortion or miscarriage.
The Empress in reverse can also indicate health
problems for you mother, or a woman in your
family.

THE EMPEROR.

A person in power is offering aid.
You move up a rung, and you make the grade.

The Emperor

The Emperor is a man in power. He is the boss or CEO of the company. He is an elected official. He is a commander in the armed forces. In the modern day I feel the Emperor can be a woman too. In the days of olde, women were not allowed to be in a position of power. In modern day women can hold positions of authority as well.

The Emperor has a way of making things happen. In the upright position he is in a position to help you, and probably will. Although the Emperor has the power, he does not abuse it. He is fair and just, and compassionate.

If Justice and the Six of Rods is nearby, the Emperor could be the judge in a legal matter. If there are many pentacles in the spread, he can help your career. If there are may cups, you may become involved with someone in powerful position.

REVERSE

The Emperor in reverse represents someone who can be somewhat of a tyrant. They are intolerant and can be cruel.

THE HIEROPHANT

A group or a society to which you belong.
Gives you some comfort to help you along.

The Hierophant

The Hierophant represents a group or organization that you belong to. Humans need to belong, it gives up a sense of identity and community. Often the Hierophant represents groups or societies that have been in place for many years. Traditions have a strong role to play.

The Hierophant can represent your church if you belong. It can represent the military, schools, hospitals, sororities and fraternities, hobbies and clubs, neighborhood associations, your nationality or ethnic group, your generation. Much depends on the surrounding cards.

If the Three of Pentacles is near, we are talking about school or college. If the Four of Rods is near, it can represent your neighborhood and community. If the Five of Cups is in the spread, you may have turned your back on your religion.

REVERSE

The Hierophant in reverse tells us that you are very unconventional. You follow the beat of your own drummer. You and are not bound by traditional roles. You may be branching out into new areas where you are not as comfortable.

THE LOVERS.

A relationship that is built upon love.
It's deep, and it's true, sent down from above.

The Lovers

The Lovers is one of the best cards in the deck.
It's what everybody strives for. To be in a close
intimate relationship. That feeling you have
when you're in love is the ultimate high. The
Lovers brings a time of great happiness, and joy.

The Lovers says that we have the whole package
physical, emotional, mental, and there is
something spiritual about it. Sometimes if there
are swords around, and if the Ace of Rods is near,
it can be just a physical connection.

If the Ace of Cups is in the spread, your new
relationship is headed for true love. If the
Two of Cups, or the Judgment card is around,
you and your Lover have been together over many
incarnations. If the Ten of Cups is there, you are
headed for marriage.

REVERSE

The Lovers in reverse tells us that the
relationship is bringing pain. You are no longer
happy together. It can also indicate that you are
still wounded from a past relationship.

THE CHARIOT.

Taking a trip, and traveling afar.
Victory's yours, or it could be your car.

The Chariot

The Chariot is known as the victory card. In any kind of competition you come out the winner. The Chariot is also about rising above a difficult situation. Either way you are victorious and come out on top.

The Chariot is also movement. If things have been stagnant, it gets moving again. Because the Chariot signals movement it also rules all forms of transportation. In the modern times the most common form of transportation is our car. Therefore if the Chariot shows up, you may be getting a new car.

If the Chariot is surrounded by pentacles, the triumph will be in the career area. If near the Four of Rods, you may be moving to a nicer house. If the Chariot comes after a lot of swords or dark cards, you will triumph over adverse conditions.

REVERSE

The Chariot in reverse tells us that you will not be the victor in this competition. It can also indicate car troubles, or a trip being cancelled.

STRENGTH.

Have patience, stay centered, you have
to be strong.
The thing that you want will be here
before long.

Strength

Patience is in order when the Strength card shows up. Strength does not refer to brute strength. She is soothing the savage beast through patience and kindness. Getting yourself into a huff will not do any good.

As a timing card, Strength tells us that there will be a delay. Because Strength is a Major Arcana greater things are at work. We do not always know why we have to wait, that is why the Strength card is two fold. You must have patience and wait for the time to be right. Because of the lion on the card, the timing may be in the time of Leo.

If Strength show up in a health reading it is a very good omen. In that case it can refer to physical strength. If the Four of Swords or The Hermit is around you may need to rest and gather your strength.

REVERSE

Strength in reverse says you are rushing things. You need to take more time and care. It can also mean that you are *not* in a position of strength.

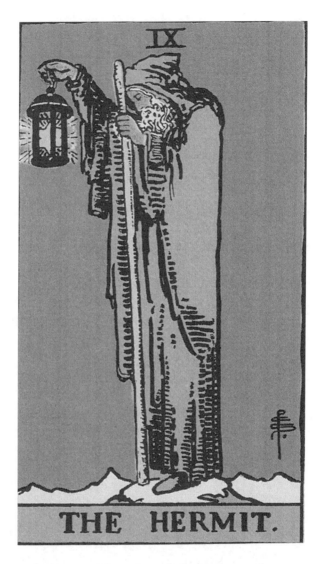

Take time to reflect, withdraw from the crowd.
Seek out wise counsel, removing the shroud.

The Hermit

The Hermit is one card that can be taken literally. You may be the Hermit, not wanting to be around other people. The rest of the spread will tell why.

Because the Hermit is a Major Arcana we know that higher forces are at work. Looking at the Hermit we see that he holds a light in his hand. To me this represents enlightenment. When we go within to seek enlightenment, we come out with a fresh perspective.

The Hermit can also be another person who gives us wise counsel. If near the Justice Card it is a lawyer. With the Three of Pentacles and the Hierophant, he may be a college professor. With the Empress, he may be a doctor.

REVERSE

The Hermit in reverse says you are not listening to wise counsel. You may want to reconsider another's advise before proceeding.

WHEEL of FORTUNE.

The wheel of life is always turning.
A fated event is often churning.

Wheel of Fortune

When the Wheel of Fortune shows up things are definitely looking up. Wheel is fate and destiny on a grand scale. Something big is happening even if you don't know it at the time. When the wheel turns up so does the tide of your affairs.

Wheel of Fortune tells us that synchronicity is at work. Synchronicity is a sign from the Universe that we are on the right path. Things just seem to go our way, we get "lucky" breaks. Being in the right place at the right time is becoming more consistent.

Wheel of Fortune with the Two of Cups shows a major fated relationship. Look to the court cards to see who the soul mate is. Wheel with the Wish Card and Ten of Pentacles can indicate a windfall perhaps from the lottery or at a casino. Wheel with the Two of Rods indicates that you are finally on the right path in life.

REVERSE

The Wheel in reverse can mean you are way off of your path. It can also refer to a fated event that will not be a happy experience for you, such as a karmic lesson.

Contracts and documents all need attending.
Deal with it now, don't leave things pending.

Justice

The most common meaning of the Justice Card is some sort of legal matter. Justice upright indicates that a legal matter will go in your favor. Court cases, signing of contracts, deeds to land. If there is a court card near, the person may be a lawyer, cop, or otherwise employed in the justice system.

Justice can also refer to karmic justice. Justice will be done on a karmic scale. If someone has wronged you, they will get what's coming to them. It's not up to you to carry out any revenge plot. The Universe in all its perfection has got it covered.

REVERSE

Justice in reverse tells us that you are being treated unfairly. A legal matter may not go in your favor.

THE HANGED MAN.

Stop and think before you proceed.
You'll get the enlightenment that you need.

The Hanged Man

The Hanged Man is often depicted in movies as a bad omen, but quite the opposite is true. The Hanged Man is not being killed or strangled. He is being enlightened. He is thinking before he speaks, or acts. He is sure that he has arrived at the right answer before proceeding.

As a timing card The Hanged Man is telling you to wait. Not a time for action. Even if you don't know why you're waiting, the timing is not right. The Hanged Man can also tell us that there is a delay, things are not happening as soon as you'd like.

If the Hanged Man is near the Star we are dealing with spiritual enlightenment. If the Hermit is near, you are interacting with a teacher or advisor.

REVERSE

The Hanged Man in reverse tells us not to wait too long, or an opportunity may pass you by. It can also say that you are not seeing things clearly.

A symbolic death is about to occur.
Things will be different from the
way they were.

Death

Death rarely means a physical death, and that should never be predicted. Death is part of the natural progression. Without Death there are no new beginnings.

Death is one of those cards where it is important to look at the surrounding cards. Whatever is behind the figure, or to the left, is what's being left behind. The cards to the right are what is coming in. Most of the time the cards behind are negative, and Death upright is a welcome change.

Death is inevitable it is the realm of Pluto. With Pluto you can do it the easy way, or you can do it the hard way. Anyway you want, change is gonna come.

REVERSE

Death in reverse is not a positive in anyway. It is stagnation, unwillingness to change. Someone cannot let the past go, therefore the new beginning eludes them.

XIV

TEMPERANCE.

Balance and harmony need be applied.
The right combination has to be tried.

Temperance

Temperance is a card of balance and harmony. Keeping things on an even keel will yield the results you are after. There are a lot of visuals on this card. Take a minute to see what is standing out to you.

Temperance is also the card of alchemy. It is getting the right combination. If you are a cook it maybe the right recipe. It could be putting together the right teams for a job, or in sports. It can refer to a collaboration with someone who you really gel with.

If the Temperance card is near the Lovers, you and your partner compliment each other and get along well. If there are many pentacles, you will find the recipe for success.

REVERSE

In reverse everything is out of whack. In a relationship there is not an equal distribution of power. If there are health issues, you may need to adjust your meds, or dosages.

You're held in bondage of your own making.
Release your fears, life's for the taking.

The Devil

The Devil is a card of false bondage. The chains are loose and easily removed, their restraints are an illusion. They are not evil, they are under the spell of the ego not the devil. The ego tries to invoke fear and limits on our limitless spirit.

In modern times when the Devil shows up it often means a drug or alcohol addiction. That is what they are in bondage to. Another not so happy alternative is the bondage is incarceration. Sometimes drug abuse and prison time go hand and hand, and the Devil would cover both. I will say jail if the chains are standing out to me.

If the Devil shows up with Moon in reverse, we are looking at a drug or alcohol problem. If the Ten of Cups in reverse is near, we are dealing with a relationship that is over, but they may not be legally divorced yet.

REVERSE

The Devil in reverse is freedom from bondage. You are finally waking up and releasing the false fears and obstacles that have held you back.

THE TOWER.

It's coming to a head, it's reached the
breaking point.
Trying to hang on right now, will only
disappoint.

The Tower

The Tower is a card of destruction. It is like a pressure cooker that explodes like a volcano erupting. The Tower is not a smooth transition. It can be violent, it tears down what was there, destroys it, so there is no resemblance of the former.

There are usually warning signs before things escalate to the point of the Tower. If you ignore the warning signs, the Universe will send in the Tower to make you change. It's another case of: we can do this the easy way or the hard way. The Tower is definitely the hard way.

The Tower with the Lovers in reverse can indicate and abusive relationship. With the Ten of Pentacles in reverse, it can mean loss of a job. With lots of swords, and the Four of Rods, you may lose your house.

REVERSE

The Tower in reverse is not much better. The destruction may not be as violent, the shock not as great, but it is still happening.

THE STAR.

Spirit is shining down on you.
Your angels and guides have you in view.

The Star

The Star is a beautiful symbol of spirit. The water is a symbol of all that is not tangible. The flow of collective consciousness from which all inspiration comes.

When the Star comes up in a spread you can be sure that you are on the right path. Spirit is with you and guiding you down the correct path, as the future cards should show. The Star can represent a specific person who has passed on.

If Star is near the Empress, a Mother or Grandmother who has passed on is near by.
If Star is near the Ace and Two of Cups, a deep spiritual love connection is coming your way.
If the Star is near a court card, that person is heaven sent.

REVERSE

The Star in reverse tells us that you are on the wrong path. We all have free will and can make our own choices. When the Star is in reverse, you are acting on your own and ignoring the Universe's guidance.

The situation is changing, things aren't
really clear.
Wait, a couple days from now the answer
will appear.

The Moon

The Moon is a card of dreams and intuition.
The Moon is fluid and ever changing. The Moon is
women, the feminine, the collective unconscious.

When the Moon shows up in the spread you have
got to rely on your intuition. The issue and hand
cannot be solved by logic. If the Moon is in the
spread you should start paying attention to your
dreams. Meditation could also be beneficial.

If the Moon is near the Star and High Priestess,
you have psychic ability. If the Two of Cups is
near, you and a lover can read each others
thoughts. The Moon with a court card can be a
timing indicator. Look for the Moon to be in the
corresponding sign.

REVERSE

The Moon in reverse is likely a drug or alcohol
problem. It can also be someone who is lying and
deceiving you. It can also be a sign of dementia,
or mental illness.

The sun is shining down on you, you're emanating
light.
You're using all your talent and gifts, and
everything's right.

The Sun

The Sun is one of the best cards in the deck.
You are shining, you're glowing, you're in your
element. You are using all your talents to the
fullest. The light of the Sun shines through you
and expands out to touch those around you.

The Sun is a card of great happiness. It can also
be a timer card. When looking for a time frame
the Sun will show us the summer months, in
particular Leo. The Sun can tell us that the
location is in a warm climate where it's always
sunny.

If the Empress or Six of Cups is near, the Sun
can represent a baby or pregnancy. If the Eight
of Cups is in the spread, you may be going on a
vacation or cruise to a sunny location.

REVERSE

The Sun in reverse is not a complete reversal, the
Sun is too powerful of a card to be diminished.
The Sun in reverse can say that you are not quite
100%. You energy is running low, you need a
recharge. You are not pregnant.

You've learned your lesson, paid your dues.
Life is open for you to choose.

Judgment

Judgment upright is a wonderful card to have. You are making real progress. You have paid your dues and learned a karmic lesson. You are ready to move on to the next level. In the Hanson Roberts deck the Judgment card distinctively points to the right. On the Rider Waite it is a little harder to discern where the horn is pointing. It is still pivotal in understanding what the lesson is all about.

If Judgment is pointing at a court card you have a deep soul connection with that person. If Judgment follows the Lovers in reverse or the Ten of Cups in reverse, you have ended a karmic relationship involving past life connections. Pointing at the Magician it is time for you to go on your own.

REVERSE

Judgment in reverse shows karmic lessons that you have yet to learn. As the saying goes: Repeating the same thing over and over again and expecting a different result is insanity. You must change your course in order to progress.

THE WORLD.

Growth beyond your wildest dreams.
The world's your oyster, so it seems.

The World

The World is called the Universe in some decks. That may be more appropriate because the World doesn't seem big enough to encompass this card. The world is bigger, better, more than you could have ever imagined when you set out on this journey.

The figure in the center of the World has everything at her disposal. All four elements, she has mastered them all. The World can indicate a world wide audience. In our modern technological age that can be achieved easier than ever before.

If the World shows up with many pentacles, you will have great wealth. With the Eight of Wands, you should start a blog. With travel cards such as the Chariot or Eight of Cups, you will be able to see the world.

REVERSE

The World in reverse is one of those situations where it is just too great a card to be bad. The World in reverse says it will still be big. It is either delayed or you just can't see it yet.

31699498R00105

Made in the USA
Middletown, DE
09 May 2016